Little Lessons from Dad

Little Lessons
from Dad

pictures by Emily Bolam

 Blue Apple Books
Brooklyn, NY

Dad

In this world you only
get one father,
and if you're really,
really lucky,
you get one like you.

You taught me
lots of stuff...

If you
s p r e a d   o u t
your peas, it looks like
you ate more.

It won't get better
any faster
if you look
under the bandage.

The clothes you leave
don't put themselves away.

Popcorn
tastes
better

from
someone
else's bag.

Bring
your
own
umbrella.

EXERCISE!

You have a lot more
respect for a bird
after you try
building a nest.

Kittens are cute,
but they have
sharp claws.

Nothing is forever,
except...

I
love
you!

Text copyright © 2003 by Harriet Ziefert
Illustrations copyright © 2003 by Emily Bolam
All rights reserved
CIP Data is available

🍎 Blue Apple Books
An affiliate of Handprint Books
413 Sixth Avenue, Brooklyn, New York 11215
www.handprintbooks.com

First Edition
Printed in China
ISBN: 1-929766-52-1

1 3 5 7 9 10 8 6 4 2

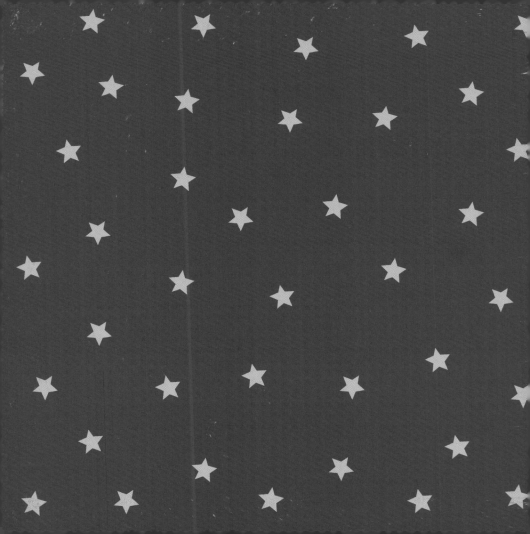